Get rid of guilt

How to effectively let go of guilt and self-doubt in 9 steps and forgive your-self

Petra Lange

CONTENT

What you can expect in this book

Guilt is a deeply human emotion that everyone has experienced (at least) once in their lives. They act as a warning signal to us that we are about to commit a wrong, that we are violating our moral code, and create an imbalance between us and one or more other people. In retrospect, they help us restore the violated balance, make amends, and learn from our mistakes.

But why do some people tend to feel inappropriately strong guilt for saying "no" just once, while others can literally walk over dead bodies without batting an eye? How do medicine and psychology explain these differences? **Where is the line between normal and pathological feelings of guilt?** And most importantly, **what can I do if I feel guilty about something I've done?**

Of course, it is difficult to give uniform recommendations for complex and individual situations - each problem deserves its own assessment and specifically tailored advice. Nevertheless, I would like to try to give you some tips on how to rationally and objectively assess your feelings of guilt, how to critically question them, and what you can try to do to free yourself from them.

To lay the groundwork for this, in this guidebook we first deal with a little theory from the fields of ethics, medicine and psycho-logy on the topics of guilt and feelings of guilt. I will then ask you some questions to help you question and become aware of your feelings, and in the explanations I will give you tips and suggestions that are as simple and practicable as possible about what you can do to restore the balance - both that in the outside world and that within you.

The root of guilt -
A bit of theory

WHAT'S TO BLAME?

Have you ever heard of **key emotions**?

In psychology, this model describes emotions or feelings that, if present in the creature in question, have proven to be a selection advantage in the course of evolution and are therefore deeply rooted in us. Although the exact localization within our gene sequence has not yet been determined, it is undisputed that these emotions are innate and thus a natural part of our human existence.

These key emotions include: **Joy and sadness, fear and disgust, anger, shame - and guilt**. [1]

Since you probably would not have chosen this book if you had no personal interest in the subject of guilt and how to deal with it, you can already rest assured: In the general consensus of current psychology, feelings of guilt are considered perfectly normal, necessary, and inevitable.

From an evolutionary point of view, feelings of guilt can even be **very useful.** After all, they would not otherwise have managed to manifest themselves in our genetic makeup in this way: They provide balance, justice in relationships, they help us avoid making mistakes or at least not making them a second time, and they make us grow in ourselves. If we find the right way to deal with them, they can be an excellent teacher, a moral compass that shows us the way to a better self.

Sounds all very positive at first. So how is it that in some situations we have the feeling that we are being eaten up from the inside by our feelings of guilt? How is it that some people are plagued by a guilty conscience as soon as they think a spiteful thought,

---

[1] https://www.k-i-e.com/die-theorie-der-grundemotionen/

while others can literally walk over dead bodies without even batting an eye? What kind of guilt is positive and helps us grow, and where is the limit beyond which guilt is only destructive?

And most importantly, how can I most effectively rid myself of guilt if I suffer from any?

> **In order to address and solve a challenge, it is of great importance to understand and become familiar with the underlying problem - often the process of becoming aware of a psychological issue is half the way to a solution.**

Therefore, we should first consider the following question: **What is "guilt"**?

If one takes a look at the dictionary, "guilt" is defined as *"a certain behavior or act by which someone violates his values and norms, a wrong committed, a moral failure or also a criminal misconduct".* [2]

If one separates this definition into its individual components, it becomes clear that **"guilt"** is **not a uniform term,** but can be applied in many situations.

• **Legal guilt** is spoken of when a certain conduct violates a law in force in that country, which is legitimized and applied there, and the person in question is

---

[2] https://www.duden.de/rechtschreibung/Schuld

prosecuted for it by the executive. It is therefore possible to be guilty of a certain conduct in one country and not be guilty in another, or to have factually violated a law, but still be considered innocent in a court of law because, for example, one cannot be proven to have committed the crime.

• **From a philosophical or moral point of view,** one is guilty as soon as one commits a violation of conscience or a moral norm. This guilt is thus far more individually defined, since although one can find a common moral denominator among many people, this is nowhere bindingly recorded and can also be interpreted and understood differently by each individual person. Accordingly, in the eye of an observer, one can be guilty by an act, while oneself or a third person would not call this a culpable act at all.

• **Other contexts in** which the term is applied are various **religions, philosophy, or in material or financial matters**.

Ultimately, however, we face a crucial problem with all these definitions: Human beings are multi-layered, and so are their actions. We try to evaluate certain deeds as positive or negative on the basis of specific criteria that we have defined. But everyone sets the criteria differently, or assigns different priorities to them - and thus arrives at a different conclusion regarding the question of guilt when evaluating an action.

To illustrate the various definitions of guilt, here is a little **thought experiment from ethics**:

> You are standing at a switch on a railroad track. On the right side, a construction worker is working on the tracks, on the left side ten. A train is approaching, the switch is set so that it will go to the left side. There is no more time to warn the workers, you would only have the time to adjust the switch so that only one person is killed instead of ten. What do you do?
>
> No matter what you decide, from a legal point of view you will be guilty, whether you move the switch or not. If you do, you are deliberately accepting the death of the worker there; if you don't, you may be construed as having failed to render assistance (at least in Germany). And the moral question is also tricky: Is it better not to actively intervene and watch ten people lose their lives, or are you more (or less) guilty if you actively choose the death of one man instead of ten?
>
> There is no right or wrong answer to these questions - you must decide based on your judgment alone.

> Think about it: What moral code do you act according to?

THE ROOT OF GUILT IN MEDICINE AND PSYCHOLOGY

If we look at the different definitions of guilt from an ethical, moral and legal point of view, we see that **being free of guilt** is, strictly speaking, an **illusion.** If one is "innocent" before the law, this does not mean that one is also morally innocent. And if one is morally innocent from the point of view of one, this is still no guarantee that one is innocent for the other - or according to one's own moral compass.

In the end, what counts for you as a person is whether you *feel* guilty. Do I have feelings of guilt after a certain act, is my guilty conscience bothering me? Or do I perhaps know that I did not act in the right way legally, but do not feel that way inside myself?

As mentioned at the beginning, guilt is one of the so-called key emotions, is anchored in our DNA and thus an innate emotion that we can never completely get rid of.

But where in the brain is the seat of these emotions located?

In **medicine, it is** not always easy to link abstract facts without an organic correlate, such as certain feelings, to exact regions in the brain. Finding the right methodology for measurement is difficult. The most proven method today is magnetic resonance imaging - a procedure in which activity in specific brain areas can be measured by applying a magnetic field.

This procedure has been used by various researchers to determine the root of guilt in the brain. German neurobiologist and philo-sophist Gerhard Roth, for example, constructed a study in the course of which he examined the brains of criminals, including murderers and rapists, for activity while they talked about their deeds. In those inmates who reported feeling remorse regarding their offense, he found increased neural excitation in the lateral orbitofrontal cortex; no such activity was measurable in those who reported having no feelings of guilt.[3] His theory was confirmed by various follow-up studies (some of which varied). [4] However, the exact reason why some of the subjects

---

[3]   https://www.nk.nomos.de/fileadmin/nk/doc/AUF-SATZ_nk_06_02.pdf

[4] https://gedankenwelt.de/in-welchem-bereich-des-gehirns-entstehen-schuldgefuehle/

were convicted of the same crime, but the intensity of the feelings of guilt and, in correlation, the brain activity of the relevant regions were reduced, has not yet been explained beyond doubt.

Another study from England also set itself the goal of finding the root of the feelings of guilt in the brain, but took as study participants not criminals, but people with increased feelings of guilt due to mental problems. The specific question was whether the activity of certain brain regions, which correlates with the presence of strong feelings of guilt, can predict the further course of the mental illness. In the course of this investigation, increased communication between the limbic system (more precisely, the cingulate gyrus and its adjacent septal region) and the anterior temporal lobe was found to be responsible for the inappropriate feelings of guilt, and indeed, in many cases, the correct prognosis was made. [5]

The aforementioned brain regions are generally responsible for processing emotions and communicate with each other via a complex regulatory circuit consisting of various messenger substances and neurotransmitters. These systems are extremely sensitive -

---

[5] https://www.aerzteblatt.de/nachrichten/64452/Depressionen-Schuldgefuehle-im-Kernspin-sagen-Rezidiv-voraus

even the smallest imbalance can shake our emotional world. And if one of the systems is disturbed, this sets other systems in motion in a domino-like manner, which also decompensate. It is therefore not surprising that **feelings of guilt and the accompanying abnormally increased activity in the brain are accompanied by a large number of concomitant diseases.**

• People who are prone to strong feelings of guilt also have a higher risk of **depression or a depressive episode at** the same time. The correlation between these two events is even so significant that strong feelings of guilt are among the optional diagnostic criteria for depression. In most cases, this is the so-called **phenomenon of "self-blaming,"** in which the patient blames himself for negative life events that, objectively speaking, he cannot influence in any way. For example, the sufferer feels guilty for having triggered the spouse's cancer because he or she "didn't care enough."

• People with **eating disorders**, especially **anorexia nervosa, are** also prone to strong feelings of guilt. Often, the mere thought of eating something (or too much) is enough to trigger agonizing feelings of guilt and shame in patients. This, in turn, is rooted in feelings of guilt that patients harbor when, looking in the mirror, they perceive their own bodies as shameful and also place the blame for this on themselves and their perceived failures.

• Also triggered by feelings of guilt are **anxiety and panic disorders**: Sufferers feel guilty about something that happened in the past and cannot cope with the fear of making the same mistake again. Avoidant, aversive behavior develops toward situations that the individuals feel they cannot handle or in which they feel this "danger" of failure. But each time they escape these situations, the fear of not being able to escape it at some point grows, setting in motion a spiral through which individuals are sucked deeper and deeper into an anxiety disorder, possibly even with panic attacks.

These are only a few examples of illnesses that are associated with feelings of guilt. Of course, the development of manifest depression or an anxiety disorder is by no means inevitable - if everyone were to develop these problems when experiencing guilt, we would probably all be affected by one of these psychological consequences. But these consequences are an indication of how seriously guilt can affect us and the power it has if we don't learn to deal with it.

Pure **psychology** approaches the problem on a different level: It looks less for the organic correlates and imbalances on a material basis of the brain, but in the interpersonal interaction, which is why its theories seem much more tangible and practical for the layman.

Here, too, the basic **mechanism behind feelings of guilt** is the **violation of a valid norm or rule** that the person concerned has internalized and that corresponds to his values, and which triggers the fear of being cast out of his social group. The feeling itself is perceived by the person as an oppressive feeling and inner turmoil, possibly coupled with feelings of shame and the desire to undo what has happened.

Some psychologists see the predisposition **to strong feelings of guilt as rooted in** our **(early) childhood experiences.**

Children are (unfortunately) very prone to feelings of guilt, even if this feeling is unjustified. They live in a world in which they cannot understand many things and therefore explain circumstances in their own way. This leads to misinterpretation of situations: For example, they see causal connections between things that happened at the same time but completely independently of each other. "Because I was born, my dad died in a car accident," is perhaps a dramatic example, but quite plausible for a child. The fact that the mother probably didn't say it that way and certainly didn't mean it doesn't matter; what matters is that it comes across to the child that way and triggers strong feelings of guilt. [6]

This approach also coincides with the depth psychological explanation according to Freud, who saw in feelings of guilt the fear of an authority. [7]

Whatever the child's feelings of guilt may be, whether it is more fear or the feeling of not having prevented an injustice or something unpleasant, in any case this situation triggers a trauma in this child, which it cannot classify and process if it does not receive appropriate support from trusted persons. Often we adults do not even recognize the problem because the contexts are completely different for us and it does not even occur to us that they could trigger feelings of guilt or failure in a child.

Now think back: Was there a situation in your childhood that triggered feelings of guilt in you, even though in retrospect you couldn't help it?

Often, as adults, we don't even really remember it. Nevertheless, unresolved traumas are something that

---

[6] https://www.erstehilfefuerdieseele.at/blog/schuldgefuhle/
[7] https://lexikon.stangl.eu/5142/schuldgefuhl

will never completely leave us. We bury them inside us, push them away from our consciousness and pretend that they no longer bother us. Until we get into a situation that, for whatever reason, we associate with the past and that stirs up old feelings again.

If as a child I felt responsible for the death of my father, who died in a car accident shortly before I was born, perhaps the death of my spouse from cancer will revive this unprocessed trauma and fuel my guilt, which I believed no longer existed. If I blamed myself for my parents' divorce because I didn't think I was good and well-behaved enough, perhaps I will blame myself for breaking up with my partner because I didn't do enough for him and to maintain the relationship. Or if, as a child, I was tormented by a guilty conscience because my parents had little time for me and I thought it was because of me, this feeling of guilt will perhaps manifest itself later towards my own children when I have to work longer hours now and then.

What we need to understand in the context of guilt in children (whether it's their own, other people's children, or thinking back to their own childhood) is that their world revolves only around them. They don't yet understand big picture issues or that they are not the center of the universe. Everything outside of what they can experience does not exist for them, or exists only in a fantasy version that we as adults with more life experience and cognitive understanding can no longer comprehend. No child will ever be able to be protected from all feelings of guilt, and accordingly that cannot be the goal. What is crucial is how feelings of guilt that have already arisen are dealt with and whether (and how) the child learns to deal with these feelings. These processing strategies that we acquire in the first years of our lives will accompany us throughout our lives, and the older we get, the more difficult it becomes to learn and manifest new strategies.

For this, it is essential to build and maintain a good relationship with the child. It doesn't matter whether it's about your own child, someone else's child, or the inner child who has not yet been able to overcome his or her traumas.

In this approach of psychology to guilt, that is the primary goal: to access and process the traumas experienced in order to then be able to build new strategies to deal with guilt and, if possible, even become free of it.

But what happens when people don't feel too much guilt, but don't feel any at all?

Psychology is also concerned with this.

As mentioned several times, guilt is a physiological process that, when present in the right measure, gives us guidance on how to act properly without harming ourselves or others.

Now let's recall back to the study in which neurobiologist and philosopher Gerhard Roth examined various offenders and found that activity in the brains differed depending on whether or not the inmates felt remorse and guilt. What is different about people who, for example, can kill another person without developing a sense of guilt? Where exactly is the difference - is it a defect at the organic level or at the psychological level? According to which moral code do they act?

To stay with the example given: Perhaps, under certain circumstances, even a person with a normally developed sense of guilt can kill another person without feeling remorse. In some situations, where we have to decide about our own life or death - i.e. act in self-defense - or to prevent harm to another person, the act of killing may be in conformity with what our ethical sense tells us to do.

In general, however, such lack of conscience is attributed more to **dissocial personality disorders** - for example, to pronounced narcissists and psychopaths[8] . However, people whose mothers regularly consumed alcohol or drugs during pregnancy also frequently show such behavior patterns.

Those affected have great difficulty fitting into social groups and norms and do not recognize structures and hierarchies. They have an increased self-esteem and believe they are above the law. They also often exhibit impulsive and aggressive behavior when things don't go their way, even to the point of a strong tendency toward violent behavior. And make no mistake about how common this problem still is in today's society!

All of these characteristics are based on that inability to feel guilt, social responsibility, or empathy, and often result in these individuals getting into trouble with the law at an early age and/or developing pronounced comorbidities, such as addiction problems or paranoid disorders. [9]

---

[8]   https://www.zeit.de/zeit-wissen/2018/01/psychologie-schlechtes-gewissen-persoenlichkeit-werte/seite-2?utm_referrer=https%3A%2F%2Fwww.google.com
[9] https://www.therapie.de/psyche/info/index/diagnose/persoenlichkeitsstoerungen/antisozial/

The problem is made more difficult by the fact that these affected persons often do not feel "mentally ill" or impaired at all (how could they, if the tormenting, negative consequences of the feelings of guilt do not occur and they see themselves as being in the right?) and, due to the lack of insight into the illness, they also lack the motivation to seek therapy or other help. As a result, help is hardly possible.

Fortunately, such disorders with diminished sense of guilt are rare on the whole. However, the fact that people harbor increased feelings of guilt is very common and therefore also the subject of this book. The good news is that the brain is changeable and able to learn how to reprogram itself to get rid of unpleasant, exaggerated feelings. Don't worry. You are not too old, too young, too smart or not smart enough, not educated enough or too intellectual. Your brain is not intentionally working against you, it has just learned certain strategies and is trying to protect you. And sometimes it overshoots the mark. And then you just have to learn to show your brain the right measure again.

"I feel guilty - now what?"

In the last chapters, we have dealt with the topic of guilt in a very theoretical way and looked at different explanatory approaches from various scientific disciplines. We have learned that "being free of guilt" is an illusion and that this state is never achieved.

Being free of guilt, on the other hand, is possible, at least in relation to certain situations. We have also illuminated that being completely free of guilt, i.e., not knowing this feeling, is a pathological mechanism that occurs in dissocial personality disorders and therefore should not be the measure of all things.

But when are feelings of guilt inappropriate? When too much and when too little? Who decides that or how can I recognize it in myself? And what can I specifically do about it?

Feelings are subjective. That is in their nature. For this reason alone, one is unlikely to find a uniform answer to the above questions. Each person will answer them differently, depending on their moral code, upbringing, resilience, personality and priorities. In the same way, each person must seek his own way to overcome his feelings of guilt.

You probably picked this book because you, too, have guilt feelings that you feel are too intense, too frequent, or too burdensome, that is, that limit you in your life in some way, and you're looking for answers. But no two situations are the same, which is why I can only share with you in this guidebook tips that have often proven effective. You are an individual. Pick the tips that appeal to you and that you feel might help you. Try them out!

Nevertheless, please remember that there is no miracle cure. These feelings are inside us, inside you, for a reason. They have manifested in the way you currently feel, and getting rid of them is a process. Give yourself time. It is work to reprogram your brain and learn new strategies, break old habit patterns and establish new routines. Be patient with yourself and don't be too hard on yourself if something doesn't work the way you thought it would or you fall back into old patterns! Be self-critical, but not ruthless with yourself! Acknowledge successes and be proud of yourself! You have already found the insight and motivation to change something about your situation, and that is already the first step in the right direction.

In the following, I will try to give you some tips that I find useful and that I hope can be useful for you as well. First of all, this includes an objective evaluation of your feelings of guilt: Based on the facts, is it reasonable and appropriate for these feelings of guilt to be bubbling up inside you? Afterwards, I will ask you ten questions and give you tips on how to answer these questions and what exactly then could be your next steps to let go of your guilt feelings piece by piece.

THE OBJECTIVE EVALUATION OF YOUR GUILT

First and foremost, I recommend that you take **a critical look at** your **feelings of guilt**.

Remember that everything you see, perceive and feel says nothing about how things are in truth. It's human to see and evaluate the world from our perspective, based on the experiences we've had in life, the upbringing we've enjoyed, and our current mood (some days we can laugh about another driver cutting us off, while the next day we might explode with anger, don't you think?). It's the same with guilt.

It depends very much on what emotional situation we are in, how guiltily we react. We project our inner attitude onto things in the outside world without realizing it. If a mishap happens to us exactly at a time when we already feel bad anyway, and we react to it with strong feelings of guilt, the brain will be able to remember this much better than a positive reaction. There is a biological reason for this: our brain wants to protect us and avoid having to relive painful situations in the future, which is why we store negative events much faster than those that went smoothly. And the less we critically question and process the event and our reaction to it afterwards, the stronger our brain will portray these negative emotions to us after some time.

In plain language this means: **Our mind manipulates us.**

In order to find out whether and to what extent it does, and whether what we feel is appropriate for the situation at hand, we have to take a **step back and look at the situation from a different, objective perspective**. From this, we can try to assess whether our feelings of guilt are normal or pathological (i.e., exaggerated or even pathological and obsessive) and how urgent the need for action is.

As is so often the case, there is **no clear definition of when feelings of guilt are no longer appropriate but pathological**. In this case, it is unfortunately unavoidable that you rely on your gut feeling after a critical and honest fact check and/or consult a trusted person who will give you an honest assessment.

What facts are relevant if you want to make a critical, fact-based judgment about whether or not your sense of guilt is appropriate?

Ask yourself the following questions and answer as honestly as you can. Take your time, write down your answers if you want. The brain processes information more intensively and can internalize it faster if we actively deal with it. In addition, you can then look at your thoughts again and again, notice changes in your thought patterns and recognize (small) successes more easily.

Assess as objectively as possible:

• **Are you guilty from a legal point of view?** Did you break any applicable law with your action?

• **Were you sane?** It is not without reason that we are considered by the law to have only limited or no culpability if, for example, we are under the influence of alcohol or drugs, if we suffer from certain mental illnesses or are under severe mental stress. Children up to the age of 14 also fall under the definition of "not capable of culpability" in this sense, as it is assumed that they cannot sufficiently foresee the consequences of their actions. Under certain circumstances, this also applies to adults.

• **Did you have any other choice?** If you act in self-defense and harm the person in question in the process, it is understandable that you develop feelings of guilt afterwards. Whether the person attacked you or not, they still hurt a human being and thus acted against your moral code. But how should you have reacted differently? Protecting yourself always takes precedence over protecting others. In this case, you would have been forced to act in this way to avoid being harmed yourself.

• **Have you violated a commitment that you consciously made?** For example, did you borrow money and promise to return it by a certain date but fail to do so? Or promised to take responsibility for someone but failed in your duty of supervision?

• **Did you act that way to assert a right of your own?** Some people are so prone to guilt that for them to say "No, I can't go out to dinner with you tonight" is unbearable. But there's nothing wrong with canceling on other people once in a while, and perhaps disappointing them, in order to take time for yourself when you need it, for example. There's nothing wrong with that, it's just human to put yourself first once in a while, as long as it's within a healthy framework and not out of excessive selfishness.

Only if you answer these questions with yes, you have factually been guilty of something and feelings of guilt are rationally appropriate. Nevertheless, these facts do not allow us to name how strong these feelings of guilt should be. Even if we are guilty of something, our feelings of guilt should not make our lives hell, but only ensure that we make amends (as far as possible) and do not commit the same mistake again. If we feel an unreasonable amount of guilt about something and can't deal with it, it's called pathological guilt, which means pathological or obsessive guilt. What is it and how do you recognize it?

Basically, feelings of guilt are pathological if they occur too often or too intensely. How often is too frequent and how much is too intense is individual. A good indicator can be whether you feel restricted in your everyday life and in your quality of life. Do your feelings of guilt keep you from doing things you would actually like to do? Or from everyday duties, such as your work? Do they limit your relationships with other people you love or care about? Do you feel them around the clock, often leaving you unable to sleep at night, or pressuring you in situations that demand your concentration? Do you feel tormented and as if you can never completely forget your feelings of guilt? Do you avoid certain situations or people in your life because they trigger or intensify feelings of guilt, and feel ashamed of them? Do you feel guilt about an event that may have happened several years ago and for which involved people have long since forgiven you? If you answer yes to one or more of these questions, your feelings of guilt may really be in a range that is no longer healthy and requires more or less urgent action.

Feelings of guilt, on the other hand, that occur only sporadically and even then are short-lived, that do not affect or burden you further, and that also require little or no reparation based on the facts, **are usually normal and healthy.** They are also uncomfortable for us and certainly not something we want to deal with, but unfortunately part of life and unavoidable. These are constructive feelings of guilt that we should learn to accept and that can be a good, faithful teacher for us in the future.

While it seems obvious, it is still important to mention for the sake of completeness: **As soon as feelings of guilt intensify to such an extent that they turn into a mental illness**, manifesting themselves, for example, in the form of a depression or an anxiety disorder, or appear as a symptom of an underlying mental illness, **they are pathological.**

As mentioned earlier, it is not uncommon in depression for patients to engage in a great deal of "self-blaming," that is, feeling responsible and blaming themselves for circumstances and events that they cannot or could not influence. Or they blame themselves for their illness because they "can't get it together." They get into a spiral of inappropriate self-doubt, self-criticism and self-hatred, of guilt, shame and despair, within which it is impossible for them to separate facts from their own feelings.

Therefore, it can be difficult for these patients to successfully take the step of critical appraisal. It is a symptom of their illness that the rational assessment of their situation no longer works. If you are affected and see this exact problem in yourself, it is incredibly important that you get help. Consult a trusted person (whom, you decide alone!) to whom you can openly describe your feelings of guilt and who will later help you to assess your position. Be as honest as possible! You do not have to be ashamed of your feelings of guilt and certainly not of your illness. I can imagine that mustering such trust with a person is not easy, but remember that we can only grow when we engage with our challenges. Even if that means showing your most vulnerable side to another person.

Let me mention at the end of this chapter: I am aware that one is often aware that one's own feelings are irrational and inappropriate, that one overreacts or emotions boil over even though there is actually no reason for them. And I am also aware that there is not always anything one can do about it. Feelings arise in us without us being asked beforehand whether we want them.

Perhaps you feel the same way about your feelings of guilt. You know that they are excessive or even outright inappropriate, that they are not doing you any good and that you need to do something about them. But you don't know where to start.

You will (probably) not get rid of your guilt feelings by explaining them as irrational. Such abstract constructs in our minds cannot be eliminated with logic alone. However, dealing with the facts logically can serve as a good starting point on your journey. Keep making the objective cornerstones clear to yourself. They are the cornerstones of your work on yourself. They are not shiftable, they stay in place, you can shimmy along between them as you learn to reprogram your brain away from guilt.

MY NINE QUESTIONS FOR YOU

Now let's go one step further. So far, we have looked at the theory behind guilt, where guilt can come from, and how to objectively assess your feelings of guilt. Most likely, this has not helped you so far to reduce them or to free yourself from them.

Even this guidebook cannot be a panacea, as much as I would like it to be. I can try to give you as concrete tips as possible in the following that can help you on your way, but you will not be able to avoid actively working on your feelings yourself. So I say to you once again: give yourself time. Be patient with yourself and allow yourself mistakes, regressions and stagnation on your path. Each of us carries our own baggage, which is why one person may find one or two steps easier than another. But you deserve to live a carefree life - without agonizing guilt or a guilty conscience. And you can achieve it. Maybe not today, maybe not tomorrow, but with enough dedication and self-confidence you will succeed.

I have packaged my tips to you in nine questions and tried to formulate them as concretely as possible, or to provide them with explanations that should make it easier for you to understand and show you options

for action. Often the feeling of helplessness is perceived as the most agonizing. I would like to give you the
opportunity to see what you have already done, to acknowledge successes you have already had and to find
new options, thus accompanying you on your way.

There is no priority or order in which you should
"work through" the questions. Proceed chronologically
or pick the questions that appeal to you the most first.
If a method doesn't appeal to you or you feel it doesn't
fit you or your situation, don't force yourself to do anything. Keep the chapter in mind and reread it at some
point; perhaps after some time something about your
situation or feelings will have changed and it can then
support you in your process. Try to approach new suggestions with as much openness as possible, rather
than categorically rejecting them. Talk to people close
to you about the tips and your own ideas that you will
surely develop while reading, you will surely learn
many more perspectives.

And maybe it will help you to keep writing down
your thoughts and reading them from time to time.
You will find that our view of things keeps changing,
from day to day, from week to week, and it will be easier for you to recognize your successes.

Who or what do you feel guilty about?

Please close your eyes for a moment. Breathe in and out deeply.

I do not know the situation you are in. I can only speculate about what triggers your feelings of guilt, and I will probably be off the mark with my assessment. People, situations, and especially feelings are too complex for anyone else to truly understand.

Now visualize the situation that makes you feel guilty. Paint a picture for yourself. Be as concrete as possible. Add details; details are what make a picture come alive and tangible.

Maybe there was a trigger. A situation you found yourself in where you didn't act as you would have thought better in hindsight. A situation in which you hurt someone - emotionally or perhaps even physically. You may also have harmed someone in some other way, taking something that was not yours to take. Or you didn't provide help when that would have been the right thing to do. Left someone alone who needed it. Made the wrong choice. Maybe you were too cowardly or maybe too direct with your words. Maybe you should have protected someone and didn't.

Or maybe it's not a specific situation that's giving you a stomachache. Maybe it's just an overall situation you find yourself in. Maybe it was a lot of small decisions that brought you to your current point, and that now add up to an uncomfortable, guilt-ridden feeling for you. Sometimes we slip into things we don't approve of without realizing it. That's okay.

It can hurt to relive such situations. Possibly even aggravate the feelings of guilt in the first moment. But we can overcome feelings only if we face them. We have to go through them, find the point of deepest pain and feel it there. Fighting the pain, resisting it, will not make it go away, but only make it worse. If we accept it, listen into it without judging it, it may not disappear, but it will become more bearable.

Once you have visualized your feelings of guilt, begin to analyze them.

In your situation, who do you feel guilty about? As we learned at the beginning, guilt is a social feeling we have toward people we have wronged and to whom we want to make amends. Do you feel guilt toward a single person? Toward a person you know and value, or perhaps even toward an unknown person? Is it purposeful guilt in that sense?

Or do you rather have collective feelings of guilt? That is, feelings of guilt towards a group of people from your environment or a collective that you may not even have in mind exactly? An example of this would be the feeling of guilt that many people feel about climate change: They feel ashamed and responsible for the destruction of the earth, but this feeling of guilt is not directed at a specific person, but at the next generation, which will suffer the consequences.

Or as a third possibility: Do you have feelings of guilt towards yourself? Are you doing or did you do something for someone else that went against your own will and now you feel you have not stood up for yourself? Have you let yourself down? Possibly entangled yourself in commitments you can't handle, but don't dare say no?

Be honest with yourself and question yourself critically. Sometimes guilt masks itself very cleverly. Sometimes we delude ourselves into feeling guilty toward someone close to us, but actually mean ourselves. For example, who doesn't know the feeling of owing something to their parents because they financed our studies? We think we have to do something well, to bring the financial imbalance back into balance, and that the achievement for this is completing this very study. That the better grades we get, the less we owe our parents. In the end, however, we owe our parents nothing. We didn't ask to come into the world, we can't choose who our parents are and what expectations they have of us.

The only person you owe from the beginning is yourself. And by completing a degree that we may not want to do at all and that will put us in a job we don't like at all, we make ourselves guilty to no one but ourselves. But this realization is hard to bear, which is why our minds want to protect us from it. It's much easier to say we owe it to our parents. That takes the responsibility off our shoulders, and for now we can pretend the problem is solved when we begin our financial independence. But, beware. This debt to ourselves will eventually catch up with us again.

Therefore, be honest: **To whom do you really feel guilty?**

How do your feelings of guilt manifest themselves?

The problem with emotions is always the same: they are very complex and multi-layered and, above all, individual. Not only in the sense that the same situation can cause different emotions in different people, depending on what experiences we have had in our lives, but the same emotion can also manifest itself in different ways in different people, depending on what type of person we are.

If something good happens to us, one person expresses his joy with shouts, cheers, and laughter, while the next person may only manage a mild smile, and again the next person may react smugly and say, "I would have been surprised if it had been different."

On the other hand, feelings of guilt may manifest themselves in me through a strong sense of shame or the need to apologize directly to the person concerned, preferably as effusively as possible, while you may no longer dare to come face to face with the person, and a third person may react physically with abdominal pain and discomfort or nausea and therefore cannot even classify their feelings of guilt as such. Just to give a few examples.

However, you are already miles ahead of the latter person in the process, because you have already recognized your feelings of guilt as such and found the motivation to work against them. From experience, this can be a lengthy process with people who tend to somatize and tend to exhibit bodily symptoms, since their access to their feelings is more complicated.

This is not to say that people who can recognize and classify their emotions as such do not perceive them physically. An emotion as a psychological manifestation always has an accompanying physical component that we can feel somewhere in the body. It is not for nothing that there are all those proverbs that describe, for example, being in love as "butterflies in the stomach" or sadness as a "lump in the throat".

Feel deeply within yourself. Where is your sense of guilt? Do you feel it in your chest? Is it a feeling of pressure, a burning, a throbbing? Or do you have it in your stomach, where it triggers an uncomfortable tugging or cramping? Does it give you palpitations or make it hard to breathe? Does it give you a headache, tinnitus, ringing in your ears, dry mouth? Does it make your knees shake? Or is it even so bad that it permanently depresses your mood, decreases your performance and drive, or triggers panic attacks? All of that is fine.

Emotions are complicated reactions in the brain that occur via the release of neurotransmitters and that can upset your body's finely balanced system quite a bit. There is nothing wrong if your body does not manage to compensate for these fluctuations. Just let it happen and notice them. Don't react with resistance, accept it. Accept your body and your feelings, unadulterated, as they are. This takes some practice.

Focus on the area where you feel the sensation most clearly and imagine breathing into that area. As if the air were flowing through your lungs directly to the feeling. Repeat this a few times and observe what happens. Observe the change in your body and within the feeling.

What have you done to get rid of your guilt?

Every person has so-called coping strategies. These are strategies that enable one to deal with stress. And feelings of guilt are emotional stress that seeks an outlet.

We build these coping strategies over the years. They are based on our early childhood experiences, on our upbringing, on our observations, on our experiences in adolescence and beyond, and partly on our intellectual capacity to assess situations and make decisions about how it would be useful to behave. We are inherently differentially resistant to stress and our coping strategies are differentially effective. These two circumstances are the basis for our varying ability to deal with stressful situations.

Have you ever asked yourself what your coping strategies are? Do you react to challenging situations more emotionally and uninhibitedly or more coolly and strategically? Both would be examples of how you deal with stressors. Are you a person who always has to talk about everything to get it off your chest, or are you good at working things out on your own?

In itself, no strategy is bad. There's a reason we adopted it at some point - at some point it was of some use to us. But perhaps it is no longer appropriate for your current situation. Maybe it's too fierce or not developed enough, or maybe it's just not effective enough.

How exactly do you deal with it when you feel guilt? What is going on in your mind?

To get rid of your guilt, you need to become an expert on your problem. You have to become aware of things. This is difficult and takes time, but if you deal with it, you will succeed. By becoming aware, I don't just mean rationally and objectively analyzing your feelings and how they function and how you evaluate them. If you deal with it enough, eventually there will come an "aha moment" when you will feel that you are not your guilty feelings and that you can control them. Just keep at it and give yourself time.

Ask yourself: Am I a person who avoids his problems, tries not to think about them, and when asked, downplays his feelings because it's not that bad? Or am I a person who can face his challenges well and be vulnerable to others? Perhaps you would like to discuss things with someone, but don't for fear of judgment - or vice versa.

What type of person you are, only you can find out, no one can answer that for you.

Think about what you have done so far, what your coping strategies have been so far. Have they helped you? If so, very good! Continue them. But if not, don't despair. That doesn't mean your strategies are bad or worthless. Think of them as something that once served you well, but has now outlived its purpose. Inwardly (or outwardly, if you like) thank your strategy and your old self for safely guiding you through many difficult situations, take the strength from it - and look forward. Look for a new strategy of action that will serve you better now.

Apart from your inner work, have you already done something on the outside, in reality, in the interpersonal sphere, to free yourself from your feelings of guilt? Have you had conversations, read up, shared experiences, apologized, or done something else? If so, what was it?

If you like, write it down. That is a success!

Whether it helped or not, you tried. You have done something!

Reflect on exactly what you felt. What helped or didn't help? Would you do it again? Or would you perhaps change something about your approach?

Specifically: For example, you apologized to the person you feel guilty about. Did you feel relieved afterwards? Did it only make things worse? Did it make you less afraid to face the person? What did that person say to you? Was the reaction positive or negative? Next time, would you apologize in a different way or perhaps phrase your apology differently?

Everything is important and can help you. There is nothing to be ashamed of, even if your strategies may not have been particularly successful so far. We are all always learning.

Are your feelings of guilt constructive or destructive?

The question about the constructiveness of your guilt partly overlaps with the question about whether your guilt is normal or pathological.

If you are already so deeply involved in your feelings of guilt that you have developed a depression or an anxiety disorder, or, conversely, if your feelings of guilt are a symptom of such an underlying disorder, the question is relatively simple to answer: they are destructive. It is the nature of these mental illnesses that the accompanying negative feelings are inappropriate to the situation and prevent you from perceiving reality as it is. This is not your fault and therefore you should not blame yourself in any case. It is more important to look ahead and find strategies for dealing with the disease and its symptoms.

In the case where your feelings of guilt are inappropriately strong (i.e., pathological) but have not yet manifested as a disease, the question is not quite so clear-cut.

Recall that the very purpose of guilt is to bring an imbalance you have caused back into balance by making amends, and to prevent you from making the same mistake again - that is, to achieve a positive end result. The purpose is not to make your life more difficult, to torment you, and thus possibly render you incapable of action. It is not to permanently rob you of your energy, which you need more urgently for other things.

Do your guilt feelings still serve this purpose? Do they cause you to act to pay your debt? Are you making them active? Or are you doing just the opposite? Do they make you passive and restrict you in your actions, make you fearful and unable to do anything?

In the second case, your feelings are destructive. They are of no use to you. Make yourself aware of this over and over again.

The important thing is that you do what you can to make amends and not repeat the mistake. Beyond that, your feelings are of no use to anyone. It is of no use to anyone if you feel bad, neither to you nor to the people around you. On the contrary, it is even more harmful to you and to those around you and the relationships you have with them. It puts a strain on you. And it can't be the point of it that you burden and possibly destroy further relationships without any purpose behind it.

What beliefs trigger your guilt and how do you get rid of them?

One more thing that we take in from an early age and carry from then on are our beliefs.

Beliefs are certain attitudes or attitudes whose existence we are often not even aware of, but which influence us every day in all our decisions, our relationships, our actions, yes, simply in our lives.

Depending on our past experiences, these beliefs can move us forward or limit us.

If you are one of those happy people who had a beautiful childhood with loving parents, who did not experience violence, and who learned that the world is a sunny place full of possibilities and beauty, you have very likely developed optimistic beliefs over time that include an intact basic trust in the world, a trust that people are basically good beings and that everything will work out as it should. You probably also have a high sense of self-efficacy, that is, the feeling that you are in control of your situation and not at its mercy.

But you may also be one of those people who have experienced a lot of negativity in their past; perhaps violence or neglect or, less dramatically, often the feeling of not being understood, of being alone and helplessly at the mercy of others. Often, people with such experiences slip more easily into beliefs that make them believe they have no say and that the needs of others are more important than their own.

To give you a better idea of what such beliefs can look like, I'll give you some examples of them below, which are more commonly associated with excessive guilt. Read carefully and react spontaneously - you may find one that is also in you:

- I am not enough.
- Everything always goes wrong for me anyway.
- I will never be as good as the others.
- I should have done much more.
- If I don't do enough for others, they won't love/appreciate me anymore.

- I don't pull myself together enough.
- I am weak.
- Something is wrong with me.
- I am powerless to change what happens to me.
- I am incompetent/inept/clumsy.
- I must not make any mistakes.
- I did not deserve it.
- I must not be selfish.
- My feelings don't matter as much as the others'.
- I do not deserve love/attention/respect from others.
- Punishment must be.

Does anything sound familiar? Or can you think of other beliefs that are stuck inside you?

It is not uncommon for us to adopt certain phrases as beliefs that someone has said to us at some point and that have burned themselves into our memory. Maybe we don't know exactly why, but they just won't let us go. Think about it: Have you heard a phrase from your parents over and over again? Or is there a phrase that you may have heard only once, but you can still remember it word for word because it was so memorable? What do you believe in?

You may have noticed that so far I have only given you negative examples of beliefs, when there are so many positive ones that you would much rather believe in.

Unfortunately, the negative attitudes are the ones that are often much more present in our lives because they are also the ones that cause us problems. After all, we tend to think a lot about what's not going well than about what's going well. So how do we get rid of the negative beliefs now?

Try to replace them with positive ones. You have certainly found some personal examples.

Take "I am not enough" as an example. Replace it with "I'm doing my best". How to do that?

As with everything, the following applies here: Practice makes perfect, and that's through repetition. Keep telling yourself that you are doing what you can. Remember situations in which you felt good and enough and needed. What situations did your presence make better, make them what they were? In what situations were you enough, just as you are? In what situations have you felt that? What people make you feel that way, that you are enough and do enough for others? Keep thinking about it, keep reinforcing that feeling. When you feel it, close your eyes and hold on to it for a moment. The more you repeat this, the more the feeling will solidify in your brain. And eventually the feeling will become the knowledge that you are doing your best. The moment will come when you have turned your belief around.

Can you make amends?

There are situations where it is possible to make things right, and situations where it is impossible. Find out which of the two you are in!

Do you have feelings of guilt because you have harmed someone? Perhaps physical harm or emotional harm? Have you perhaps said something you didn't mean and hurt someone badly? Have you put someone through too much, causing your relationship to become unbalanced? Do you owe someone financially or materially because you may have taken something you weren't entitled to? Have you perhaps had to give notice to a good co-worker who you know is in financial trouble right now? Have you perhaps cheated or lied to someone?

If you find yourself in such a situation where you have harmed another person in some way, whether knowingly or unintentionally, consider how you can repay your debt.

In material or financial matters, this is relatively simple: pay off those debts as best you can. If you can't do that at the moment, talk to your creditors and negotiate a plan that is acceptable to both parties and that shows both sides that you are aware of your debts and that you are willing to pay them. In these matters, communication is everything! Even if you have misappropriated the property and the other party doesn't even know about it, for the sake of your conscience, you should talk to the other person about it. It is quite possible that the person will react angrily or disappointed at the first moment. Therefore, think about a fair offer to make beforehand and leave room for action so that your counterpart feels appreciated and taken seriously. You will be surprised how much open communication can ease your conscience and also the objective situation! And give the other person time to formulate their demands and respond to them - within a framework that is also tolerable for you.

For example, do you feel guilty towards your family because you don't have enough time for them? Do you work far too much and at the same time feel that you cannot fulfill your roles towards your children or your partner? Many people feel this way. Pay attention! With the belief of not being enough and not doing enough, you are stumbling very purposefully into burnout! Again, consider where your priorities lie and communicate openly with your family! Is it necessary for you to work so much? What's more important, time with your family or earning a few hundred extra dollars a month? You will not be able to buy time with any money in the world and certainly not the love of other people. Make yourself aware of that! Maybe you can find a compromise that gives both sides a good feeling: for example, make a day that is reserved only for your most important people. On that day, the cell phone stays off, appointments are moved around that day, you do exactly what you want to do, and you don't let anyone take that day away from you. Make a list of things you've always wanted to do with your favorite people, and pick something from it each week. Don't resent the fact that you haven't been able to do it so far. It doesn't help anyone to live in the past and regret things. Learn from it and do better in the future!

But you may also owe something to someone with whom you cannot make amends. Perhaps the person has already passed away, or the person has done something so wonderful for you that you cannot make it up to them. Let's take the example that your sister donated a kidney to you and you were able to overcome your illness only because of it, but now she herself has become ill because of it.

Do not forget yourself. You are aware that you owe that person something. Learn to accept that life is not always fair, nor does it always have to be. Terrible things happen and also things that seem quite unfair to us at first glance. But does it change anything if we feel bad about things we can't change? The situation remains the same. And in the worst case, our feeling of guilt for this thing is rather a hindrance, because it blocks and paralyzes us and prevents us from drawing the positive out of the situation. Because that's exactly what you should do: look for the good in things! Even if it does not seem so, everything, yes really everything, has several sides. There is something positive in every misfortune. Find the positive, however small it may be, and focus on it! Maybe your sister is sick now because she wanted to save your life. But she knew beforehand that there was a risk of that, and she went for it. For you. Don't focus on your guilt about it, but focus on the fact that your sister showed her love to you in this way. Be grateful for that and tell her so! Show her your appreciation, because no misfortune happens in vain.

And the same advice applies if you feel guilty about yourself because you just can't say no, for example: There's nothing wrong with refusing or turning down requests from other people. Value yourself and your time more! Be grateful that you have managed to say no. In doing so, you have given yourself a great gift - and there is nothing to be ashamed of!

Who can you talk to about your feelings?

Even with the previous questions, my advice and experience always boiled down to one thing: communication!

Language is a wonderful gift we have received from evolution. We should use our intellect and this skillful way of expression to give an outlet to our feelings. Who is eligible for this?

Think about it: who is it that is closest to you? Which person or persons do you trust most in this world? Who can you go to when you need someone to talk to? Which person makes you feel like you understand them right away?

Talk to this person. Take them into your confidence.

Often we are afraid to talk about feelings, especially when it comes to negative feelings. We think that it makes us vulnerable, that it is something to be ashamed of, because it exposes our shortcomings so openly, because it makes us admit that we are not perfect.

It's brave to admit that. And it is good. It makes us human toward others. Our leap of faith also makes it easier for the other person to admit his or her mistakes. It takes the pressure out of relationships to have to meet the demands of the other person.

Or talk to yourself. Maybe by writing it down. Or maybe by actually talking to yourself. This may sound strange at first, but by writing things down or saying them out loud, we firstly get rid of them and secondly it helps us not to lose the thread. Often, it is only after we have spoken out a thought that the idea for the next thought comes to us because we have freed ourselves from the previous one. Try it out!

Why can't you forgive yourself?

When a person wrongs us, we can either resent him eternally or forgive him. When we wrong another person and feel guilty, we cannot decide whether the other person will forgive us, but we can forgive ourselves.

Let go of perfectionism! Of course, we would all prefer to be without faults and never harm another person, but sometimes we find ourselves in a situation where there is no other way or we act rashly.

Making mistakes is human. You know that. So why is it so hard for us to admit mistakes to ourselves?

We often find it easier to forgive others than ourselves. This is because we are usually our own harshest critics. We demand too much of ourselves, set our standards too high, and will thereby disappoint ourselves again and again because we can never live up to them. We think that everyone else, especially the people who are important to us, would expect this or that from us, not realizing that it is mainly ourselves whose expectations we are trying to fulfill.

Perhaps you are one of those people whose parents had very high expectations of them. Perhaps, as a child, you often felt that you had to perform for your parents' love or that you didn't deserve love if you didn't do anything for it. Perhaps this has continued until now, into adulthood. Maybe you still often have the feeling that your fellow human beings only appreciate you if you do something for them and you have feelings of guilt because you think what you do is too little or not good enough.

Be honest: Is this the kind of relationship you want to have with the people around you? With your parents, your partner or your friends? Shouldn't love or friendship be about accepting a person for who they are? Do you want to be dependent on the approval of others?

It may be that not all people will understand you if you do things your way, or that some will have to get used to it. But the people who really care about you and who don't see you as just a means to an end will stick with you and support you. Don't feel guilty about allowing yourself to be yourself!

What if they can't accept it?

Then it has not been a real love or friendship either. You will find that people will respect you if you demand what is rightfully yours from time to time.

So the people around you are not your harshest critics, you are.

When we have made a mistake, we often fall into a compulsion to justify ourselves: We think we have to explain how this mistake could have happened - to others and to ourselves. Often we can rationally explain how it happened and still feel guilty. But you are not accountable to anyone! It only throws you into a defensive posture where you quickly feel attacked, which in turn tempts us to react passively(-aggressively) and with counter-accusations. Say clearly that you made a mistake and that you are aware of it, that you will try to make amends and that you have learned from it.

Get a grip on your perfectionism! Realize that you too are allowed to make mistakes. And yes, even big mistakes! Forgive yourself and don't hold grudges! It is not a weakness to make mistakes. And it is even a special strength if you are able to admit mistakes and apologize. Learn from your mistakes and don't make them a second time.

What can I learn from my mistake?

You have now dealt with what you did wrong, whether your feelings of guilt are appropriate, what mechanisms are behind the fact that your feelings of guilt are as pronounced as they are, and how you can make up for your mistake. Finally, the question remains: What can you take away from this for the future?

As mentioned earlier, you should try to find the positive in your situation and focus on that. You are intelligent and can think cognitively. You should use that!

You know the situation that led you to your action and ultimately to your feelings of guilt. Were there warning signs that something like this would happen? If so, what were they? Sensitize your senses to this, always critically question your actions and your feelings. Should you slip into something similar again, you now have the chance to recognize it early on and pull the emergency brake. Take those around you into your confidence when you are unsure of how to act. Get other perspectives and be open!

And if you do find yourself in a similar situation again, use the experience you have already gained to perhaps react differently next time. You now know your behavior patterns and your trigger points. Your awareness of this can be of benefit to you if you manage to break through these patterns, take a breath and not act impulsively.

Sometimes you have to make difficult decisions despite all prudence. Learn to communicate this! Conversation skills can be learned and the more often you have difficult conversations, the easier it will be for you. Paradoxical, isn't it?

Write down everything you can think of that you can learn from it. Focus on it. Read it over and over and honor it when you were in a situation where what you learned could be useful to you. Everything we do and learn has a purpose. We just have to find it!

A brief summary

Feelings of guilt are normal and desired to give us moral guidance in our lives. Nevertheless, in the wrong context, they can become agonizing and unpleasant and even manifest themselves in mental illness.

When that happens, it's time to act. We have to learn to lower the standards we set for ourselves, admit to mistakes and let go of perfectionism. And then see how we can make up for our mistake. The key to this lies in communication.

Be patient, it's a long road. But it's worth taking it to be able to live the carefree life you deserve!